Bibliographical Series
of Supplements to 'British Book News'
on Writers and Their Work

★

GENERAL EDITOR
Bonamy Dobrée

¶ George Herbert was born at Montgomery Castle on 3 April 1593. He died on 3 March 1633 and was buried at Bemerton, Wiltshire.

GEORGE HERBERT
after an engraving by R. White which first
appeared in Izaac Walton's *Life*, 1670, and
in the 1674 edition of *The Temple*.

GEORGE HERBERT

by T. S. Eliot

PUBLISHED FOR
THE BRITISH COUNCIL
and the NATIONAL BOOK LEAGUE
by LONGMANS, GREEN & CO.

LONGMANS, GREEN & CO. LTD.,
48 Grosvenor Street, London, W.1.
Railway Crescent, Croydon, Victoria, Australia
Auckland, Kingston (Jamaica), Lahore, Nairobi

LONGMANS SOUTHERN AFRICA (PTY) LTD.
Thibault House, Thibault Square, Cape Town,
Johannesburg, Salisbury

LONGMANS OF NIGERIA LTD.
W.R. Industrial Estate, Ikeja

LONGMANS OF GHANA LTD.
Industrial Estate, Ring Road South, Accra

LONGMANS GREEN (FAR EAST) LTD.
443 Lockhart Road, Hong Kong

LONGMANS OF MALAYA LTD.
44 Jalan Ampang, Kuala Lumpur

ORIENT LONGMANS LTD.
Calcutta, Bombay, Madras
Delhi, Hyderabad, Dacca

LONGMANS CANADA LTD.
137 Bond Street, Toronto 2

First Published in 1962
© T. S. Eliot 1962

Printed in Great Britain by
F. Mildner & Sons, London, E.C.1

GEORGE HERBERT

I

THE family background of a man of genius is always of interest. It may show evidence of powers which blaze forth in one member, or it may show no promise of superiority of any kind. Or it may, like that of George Herbert, show distinction of a very different order. There is a further reason for knowing something of the ancestry of George Herbert: it is of interest to us because it was important to him.

The family of Herbert was, and still is, notable among the British aristocracy. I say British rather than English, because one branch of the family, that to which the poet belonged, had established itself in Wales and had intermarried with Welsh landed families. The Herberts lay claim to being of Norman-French origin, and to having been land-holders since the Norman conquest. At the time of the Wars of the Roses the Herberts of Wales had supported the Yorkist cause; but after the battle of Bosworth they transferred their allegiance to the new monarch, the Lancastrian Henry Tudor, himself a Welshman on his father's side, who ascended the throne as Henry VII. Under the new dynasty the Herberts continued to flourish. Henry VII was determined to exert in Wales the same authority that he enjoyed in England—a control to which the local chieftains of Wales were not accustomed. Among those Welshmen of position and authority who supported and advanced King Henry's law and order in Wales was Sir Richard Herbert of Montgomery Castle. Montgomery lies in North Wales; in the South another Herbert was (and is) Earl of Pembroke; and still another branch of the family is represented by the Earl of Carnarvon.

George Herbert's ancestors and kinsmen were active both in the service of the King and in local affairs. Their rank was among the highest. Several of the family were distinguished for their courage, their prowess in war and duel and

5

their astonishing feats of arms. An exceptional race, but giving no indication of literary tastes and ability before the time of George Herbert and his brother Edward. That two poets, brothers, should appear in a family so conspicuous for warlike deeds, administrative gifts and attendance at Court, can only be accounted for by the fact that their mother, the wife of Sir Richard Herbert of Montgomery, was a woman of literary tastes and of strong character and of exceptional gifts of mind as well as beauty and charm. She was Magdalen, daughter and heiress of Sir Richard Newport, a wealthy landowner in Shropshire.

George Herbert was born in 1593. Three years later his father died, leaving the mother with ten children, seven boys and three girls. Edward was the eldest son; the younger sons would have, of course, to make their own way in life—presumably, as other Herberts had done, in the wars or in some public service—but Lady Herbert's standards were high and she was determined to give them all a good education. The eldest, Edward, the other poet of the family and the heir to the estates, was thirteen and already an undergraduate at Oxford when his father died. At fifteen Edward was married off to an heiress (a Herbert of another branch) but continued at Oxford, where his mother moved her family to be near him and to supervise his education. There she made friends, and even held a kind of salon, among the more brilliant of the learned dons.

It is worth while to say something of Edward Herbert, the eldest brother, not merely to mention his poetry but to point the striking contrast between the two gifted brothers. Edward was ambitious to live abroad, to enjoy court life in foreign capitals and to engage in rather dilletante diplomacy; and to this end he learned French, Italian and Spanish. He seems to have been a man of great physical strength, and was noted for his address at sports and success in love-making: in short, he was a man of abounding vitality. He was later raised to the peerage as Lord Herbert of Cherbury, by which name he is known as author of at least two very fine poems familiar to readers of anthologies. He was not only a poet, but something of a philosopher, and entertained distinctly heretical views in religious matters. On the other hand, John Donne spoke well of him, and Ben Jonson was a friend and correspondent. For he enjoyed the society of men of letters, among whom he moved as an equal as well as among the courtiers of Europe and among ladies and gentlemen of fashion. In Edward the characteristic traits of the Herberts and some of the particular traits of Magdalen Herbert, his mother, appear to have been combined. In George, of frailer constitution and contemplative mind, we seem to find more of Magdalen; yet he was as proudly conscious of being a Herbert as any other Herbert, and at one period had the family inclination to life in the world of public affairs.

By far the most important for our study of George Herbert, of the men of letters and the scholars who delighted in the company of Magdalen Herbert, was John Donne. He was enough older in years to have the admiration of the younger man and to influence him: he was enough beneath Lady Herbert in rank to be almost a protégé. The friendship between Donne and Lady Herbert is commemorated in one of Donne's best known and most loved poems, 'The Autumnal', in which is found the couplet which every lover of Donne's poetry knows by heart:

> No Spring, nor Summer Beauty hath such grace
> As I have seen in one Autumnal face.

To the influence of Donne's poetry upon that of Herbert we shall return presently. Meanwhile it is in place to provide a brief survey of Herbert's life and a sketch of his character.

At the age of twelve George Herbert was sent to Westminster School, where he became proficient in the usual disciplines of Latin and Greek, and gained also—what is equally important for mention here—an advanced practice in music: not only in the choral singing for which that famous school was well known because of its association with the services in Westminster Abbey, but also with a difficult instrument—the lute. If we remember Herbert's knowledge of music, and his skill at the instrument, we appreciate all the better his mastery of lyric verse. From Westminster he went on to Trinity College Cambridge, being one of three boys of Westminster School who were given scholarships to that College at that time.

At Westminster School Herbert had an exemplary record. The relation of the school to the Abbey had also familiarised him with the church offices, in which the boys took part. (Their close attention to the sermon was ensured by the requirement that they should afterwards compose a summary of it in Latin.) At the university Herbert was equally forward; sober and staid in his conduct and diligent in his studies, he was given particular attention by the Master. It was said of him, however, that he was careful to be well, even expensively dressed; and that his attitude towards his fellow undergraduates of lower social position was distant, if not supercilious. Even Isaac Walton (his most nearly contemporary biographer) who tends to emphasise Herbert's saintliness, admits that Herbert, at this stage of his life, was very much aware of the consideration which he thought due to his exalted birth.

At the age of twenty-three Herbert was made a Fellow of his own college of Trinity. He began by instructing the younger undergraduates in Greek grammar; later he taught rhetoric and the rules of oratory. His health was never good; and the climate of Cambridge was somewhat harsh for a young man of frail constitution. His income as Fellow and Tutor was eked out by a small allowance from his brother Edward (the head of the family) and occasionally by gifts from his step-father. For his mother had, in middle age, married again, and was now the wife of Sir John Danvers. But Herbert's poor health meant doctors' bills and occasional absences from Cambridge; as a learned scholar of an active and curious mind he needed constantly to purchase books, and books were expensive, especially those which had to be imported from the continent. He therefore sought to improve his finances, and at the same time attain a position of considerable dignity, by obtaining appointment as Public Orator to the University.

Herbert had not yet formed the design of passing his life as a country parson. Indeed, the post of Public Orator was one which would bring him into the great world and even into contact with the court of James I. He achieved his aim; and during his tenure of this office acquired an extensive acquaintance, which his family connections and his own wide sympathies helped to enlarge. He greatly admired Sir Francis Bacon, a man of a type of mind very different from his own; another elder friend with whom he was on affectionate terms was the saintly Bishop Lancelot Andrewes. Nor did a wide divergence of religious attitude and belief diminish the warm regard between him and his elder brother Edward.

A Fellow of a College was expected to take holy orders in the Church of England within seven years of his appointment, or resign his Fellowship. Herbert was, like his mother, a practising and devout Anglican, but at this time his ambition looked toward the world of Court and Government. His violent attack, in the form of a Latin thesis, upon the Puritan position in the person of one of its most outrageous zealots, Andrew Melville, was his only sortie into religious controversy; though undoubtedly wholly sincere, Herbert probably aimed at winning the approval of King James. He would certainly have liked public office, but had neither the wiles of ingratiation, nor the means or the wish to buy his way in. His next step was to become Member of Parliament for Montgomery—an election which came to him almost as a matter of course as a member of the Herbert family. But this period of his life was not marked by success: two great noblemen of whose patronage he felt assured died, and the death of King James himself, in the following year, seems to have left him with little hope of a Secretary-ship of State.

It was necessary to review this much of Herbert's early life to make the point that Herbert, though from childhood a pious member of the Anglican Church, and a vigorous opponent of the Puritans and Calvinists, felt no strong vocation to the priesthood until his thirty-first year. There were at least four persons in his life who may, by precept or example, have influenced him to this decision. His mother, to whom he was devotedly attached, was, we know, a woman not only of strong character, but of great piety. Two friends much older than himself have already been mentioned: Dr. John Donne and Bishop Andrewes. And finally, there was his dear friend Nicholas Ferrar of Little Gidding, an exemplar of High Churchmanship, whose domestic life approached that of a religious community. To Ferrar it was that he consigned, upon his death, the manuscript collection of verse upon which his fame is founded, the collection *The Temple* which we should not know had Ferrar not chosen to publish it; this he did in the same year in which Herbert died.[1]

[1] Four editions of *The Temple* appeared within three years of its first publication; its popularity continued to the end of the century. In the eighteenth century Herbert's poems were generally disparaged: Cowper, for instance, though he found in them a strain of piety which he admired, regarded them as 'gothick and uncouth', and this was the universal opinion of that age. The restoration of Herbert's reputation was begun by Coleridge who, in a letter to William Collins, dated 6 December 1818, writes: '. . . I find more substantial comfort now in pious George Herbert's 'Temple' which I used to read to amuse myself with his quaintness—in short, only to laugh at—than in all the poetry since the poems of Milton. If you have not read Herbert, I can recommend the book to you confidently. The poem entitled 'The Flower' is especially affecting; and, to me, such a phrase as 'and relish versing' expresses a sincerity, a reality, which I would unwillingly exchange for the more dignified 'and once more love the Muse' &c. And so, with many other of Herbert's homely phrases.' (Letters, vol. IV, edited by Earl Leslie Griggs, 1959.)

Writing to Lady Beaumont in 1826, Coleridge says: 'My dear old friend Charles Lamb and I differ widely (and in point of taste and moral feeling this is a rare occurrence) in our estimate and liking of George Herbert's sacred poems. He greatly prefers Quarles—nay he dislikes Herbert.' (The Letters of Charles Lamb, edited by E. V. Lucas, vol. I, 1935.)

Herbert's mother died in 1626. George Herbert was for a time a guest in the house of his step-father's elder brother, Lord Danvers, and in 1629, having already taken holy orders, he married Jane Danvers, the daughter of a cousin of Lord Danvers. It was a happy marriage. Six years after Herbert's death, his widow married Sir Robert Cook. In her widowhood, Isaac Walton says:

> . . . She continued mourning, till time and conversation had so moderated her sorrows, that she became the happy wife of Sir Robert Cook of Highnam in the County of Gloucester, Knight. And though he put a high value on the excellent accomplishments of her mind and body; and was so like Mr. Herbert, as not to govern like a Master, but as an affectionate Husband; yet she would even to him take occasion to mention the name of Mr. George Herbert, and say that name must live in her memory, till she put off mortality.

George Herbert died of consumption at the age of forty. For the last years of his life he had been Rector of the parish of Bemerton in Wiltshire. That he was an exemplary parish priest, strict in his own observances and a loving and generous shepherd of his flock, there is ample testimony. And we should bear in mind, that at the time when Herbert lived, it was most unusual that a man of George Herbert's social position should take orders and be content to devote himself to the spiritual and material needs of a small parish of humble folk in a rural village. From Walton's *Life* I must quote one anecdote:

> In another walk to *Salisbury*, he saw a poor man, with a poorer horse, that was fall'n under his Load; they were both in distress, and needed present help; which Mr. *Herbert* perceiving, put off his Canonical Coat, and help'd the poor man to unload, and after, to lead his horse: The poor man blest him for it: and he blest the poor man; and was so like the *good Samaritan* that he gave him money to refresh both himself and his horse; and told him, *That if he lov'd himself, he should be merciful to his Beast.* Thus he left the poor man, and at his coming to his musical friends at *Salisbury*,

they began to wonder that Mr. *George Herbert* which us'd to be so trim and clean, came into the company so soyl'd and discompos'd; but he told them the occasion: And when one of the company told him, *He had disparag'd himself by so dirty an employment;* his answer was, *That the thought of what he had done, would prove Musick to him at Midnight; and that the omission of it would have upbraided and made discord in his Conscience, whensoever he should pass by that place; for, if I be bound to pray for all that be in distress, I am sure that I am bound so far as it is in my power to practise what I pray for. And though I do not wish for the like occasion every day, yet let me tell you, I would not willingly pass one day of my life without comforting a sad soul, or shewing mercy; and I praise God for this occasion:* And now let's tune our instruments.

In this context is worth mention a prose treatise of Herbert's entitled *A Priest to the Temple Or The Country Parson His Character etc.* In this treatise he sets forth the duties and responsibilities of the country parson to God, to his flock, and to himself; and from what we know of Herbert we can be sure that he practised, and always strove to practise, what he here prescribes to other priests. The story of the poor man and his horse is all the more touching when we read that the Parson's apparell should be

plaine, but reverend, and clean, without spots, or dust, or smell; the purity of his mind breaking out, and dilating it selfe even to his body, cloaths, and habitation.

We are told elsewhere in the same treatise that a priest who serves as domestic chaplain to some great person is not to be

over-submissive, and base, but to keep up with the Lord and Lady of the house, and to preserve a boldness with them and all, even so farre as reproofe to their very face, when occasion calls, but seasonably and discreetly.

The pride of birth natural to Herbert is transformed into

the dignity of the Servant of God. The parson, he continues, should be a man of wide reading: Herbert mentions the Church Fathers and the Scholastics, and tells us that the parson should be attentive to later writers also. The parson must give careful attention to his sermon, taking due account of the needs and capacities of his parishioners, and keeping their attention by persuading them that his sermon is addressed to this particular congregation and to one and all of them. And he should, especially when visiting the sick, or otherwise afflicted, persuade them to particular confession, 'labouring to make them understand the great good use of this antient and pious ordinance'.

We are not to presume, however, that George Herbert was naturally of a meek and mild disposition. He was, on the contrary, somewhat haughty; proud of his descent and social position; and, like others of his family, of a quick temper. In his poems we can find ample evidence of his spiritual struggles, of self-examination and self-criticism, and of the cost at which he acquired godliness.

I struck the board, and cry'd, No more.
　　　　I will abroad.
What? shall I ever sigh and pine?
My lines and life are free; free as the rode,
　　Loose as the winde, as large as store.
　　　　Shall I be still in suit?
Have I no harvest but a thorn
To let me bloud, and not restore
What I have lost with cordiall fruit?
　　　　Sure there was wine
Before my sighs did drie it: there was corn
　　Before my tears did drown it.
　　Is the yeare onely lost to me?
　　　　Have I no bayes to crown it?
No flowers, no garlands gay? all blasted?
　　　　All wasted?
Not so, my heart: but there is fruit
　　　　And thou hast hands.

> Recover all they sigh-blown age
> On double pleasures: leave thy cold dispute
> Of what is fit and not. Forsake thy cage,
>   Thy rope of sands,
> Which pettie thoughts have made, and made to thee
>   Good cable, to enforce and draw,
>   And be thy law,
> Whilst thou didst wink and wouldst not see.
>   Away; take heed;
>   I will abroad.
> Call in thy deaths head there: tie up thy fears.
>   He that forbears
>   To suit and serve his need
>   Deserves his load.
> But as I rav'd and grew more fierce and wilde
>   At every word,
> Me thoughts I heard one calling, *Child*!
>   And I reply'd, *My Lord*.

(The Collar)

To think of Herbert as the poet of a placid and comfortable easy piety is to misunderstand utterly the man and his poems. Yet such was the impression of Herbert and of the Church of England given by the critic who wrote the introduction to the World's Classics edition of Herbert's Poems in 1907. For this writer, the Church of England, in Herbert's day as well as in his own, is typified by a peaceful country churchyard in the late afternoon:

> Here, as the cattle wind homeward in the evening light, the benign, white-haired parson stands at his gate to greet the cowherd, and the village chimes call the labourers to evensong. For these contented spirits, happily removed from the stress and din of contending creeds and clashing dogmas, the message of the gospel tells of divine approval for work well done. . . . And among these typical spirits, beacons of a quiet hope, no figure stands out more brightly or more memorably than that of George Herbert.

This rustic scene belongs to the world of Tennyson and Dickens; but no more to the world of George Herbert than

to our world to-day. It is well that the latest World's Classics
edition (the text based on that established by F. E.
Hutchinson) has a new introduction by a learned and sensi-
tive critic, Miss Helen Gardner. The earlier introduction
gave a false picture both of Herbert and his poetry, and of
the Church itself in an age of bitter religious conflict and
passionate theology: it is worth quoting in order to point
out how false a picture this is.

II

The poems on which George Herbert's reputation is based
are those constituting the collection called *The Temple*.
About *The Temple* there are two points to be made. The
first is that we cannot date the poems exactly. Some of
them may be the product of careful re-writing. We cannot
take them as being necessarily in chronological order: they
have another order, that in which Herbert wished them to
be read. *The Temple* is, in fact, a structure, and one which
may have been worked over and elaborated, perhaps at
intervals of time, before it reached its final form. We cannot
judge Herbert, or savour fully his genius and his art, by any
selection to be found in an anthology; we must study *The
Temple* as a whole.

To understand Shakespeare we must acquaint ourselves
with all of his plays; to understand Herbert we must
acquaint ourselves with all of *The Temple*. Herbert is, of
course, a much slighter poet than Shakespeare; nevertheless
he may justly be called a major poet. Yet even in anthologies
he has for the most part been underrated. In Sir Arthur
Quiller-Couch's *Oxford Book of English Verse*, which was
for many years unchallenged in its representative character,
George Herbert was allotted five pages—the same number
as Bishop King and much less than Robert Herrick, the
latter of whom, most critics of to-day would agree, is a poet
of very much slighter gifts. For poetic range Herbert was

commonly considered more limited than Donne; and for intensity he was compared unfavourably with Crashaw. This is the view even of Professor Grierson, to whom we are greatly indebted for his championship of Donne and those poets whose names are associated with that of Donne.

And here we must exercise caution in our interpretation of the phrase 'the school of Donne'. The present writer once contemplated writing a book under that title; and lately the title has been used by a distinguished younger critic for a study covering the same ground. The phrase is legitimate and useful to designate that generation of men younger than Donne whose work is obviously influenced by him, but we must not take it as implying that those poets who experienced his influence were for that reason lesser poets. (Professor Grierson, indeed, seems to consider Andrew Marvell the greatest, greater even than Donne.) That Herbert learned directly from Donne is self-evident. But to think of 'the school of Donne', otherwise 'the metaphysical poets', as Donne's inferiors, or to try to range them on a scale of greatness, would be to lose our way. What is important is to apprehend the particular virtue, the unique flavour of each one. Comparing them with any other group of poets at any other period, we observe the characteristics which they share: when we compare them with each other, their differences emerge clearly.

Let us compare a poem by Donne with a poem by Herbert; and as Herbert's poetry deals always with religious matter, we shall compare two religious sonnets. First, Donne:

> Batter my heart, three person'd God; for, you
> As yet but knocke, breathe, shine, and seeke to mend;
> That I may rise, and stand, o'erthrow mee', and bend
> Your force, to breake, blowe, burn and make me new.
> I, like an usurpt towne, to'another due,
> Labour to 'admit you, but Oh, to no end,
> Reason your viceroy in mee, mee should defend,
> But is captiv'd, and proves weake or untrue.

Yet dearely' I love you,' and would be loved faine,
But am betroth'd unto your enemie:
Divorce mee, 'untie, or break that knot againe;
Take mee to you, imprison mee, for I
Except you 'enthrall mee, never shall be free,
Nor ever chast, except you ravish mee.

And here is George Herbert:

Prayer (1)

Prayer the Churches banquet, Angels age,
   Gods breath in man returning to his birth,
   The soul in paraphrase, heart in pilgrimage,
The Christian plummet sounding heav'n and earth;
Engine against th' Almightie, sinners towre,
   Reversed thunder, Christ-side-piercing spear,
   The six-daies world transposing in an houre,
A kinde of tune, which all things heare and fear;
Softnesse, and peace, and joy, and love, and blisse,
   Exalted Manna, gladnesse of the best,
   Heaven in ordinarie, man well drest,
The milkie way, the bird of Paradise,
     Church-bels beyond the starres heard, the souls bloud,
     The land of spices; something understood.

The difference that I wish to emphasise is not that between the violence of Donne and the gentle imagery of Herbert, but rather a difference between the dominance of intellect over sensibility and the dominance of sensibility over intellect. Both men were highly intellectual, both men had very keen sensibility: but in Donne thought seems in control of feeling, and in Herbert feeling seems in control of thought. Both men were learned, both men were accustomed to preaching—but not to the same type of congregation. In Donne's religious verse, as in his sermons, there is much more of the *orator*: whereas Herbert, for all that he had been successful as Public Orator of Cambridge University, has a much more intimate tone of speech. We do not know what Herbert's sermons were like; but we can conjecture that in addressing his little congregation of rustics, all of whom he knew personally, and many of whom must have received both spiritual and material comfort from him and from his wife, he adopted a more homely style. Donne was accustomed to addressing large congregations (one is tempted to call them 'audiences') out of doors at Paul's Cross, Herbert only the local congregation of a village church.

The difference which I have in mind is indicated even by the last two lines of each sonnet. Donne's

> ... for I
> Except you'enthrall me, never shall be free,
> Nor ever chast, unless you ravish mee

is, in the best sense, *wit*. Herbert's

> Church-bels beyond the starres heard, the souls bloud,
> The land of spices, something understood

is the kind of poetry which, like

> magic casements, opening on the foam
> Of perilous seas, in faery lands forlorn

may be called *magical*.

Of all the poets who may be said to belong to 'the school of Donne', Herbert is the only one whose whole source of inspiration was his religious faith. Most of the poetry upon which rests the reputation of Donne is love poetry, and his religious verse is of a later period in his life; his reputation, and his influence upon other poets would have been as great had he written no religious poetry at all. Richard Crashaw, who had himself frequented the community of Nicholas Ferrar at Little Gidding before his conversion to the Church of Rome, might still have been a notable poet had he written no religious verse—even though his devotional poems are his finest. Herbert, before becoming Rector of Bemerton, had never been a recluse: he had, in his short life, wide acquaintance in the great world, and he enjoyed a happy marriage. Yet it was only in the Faith, in hunger and thirst after godliness, in his self-questioning and his religious meditation, that he was inspired as a poet. If there is another example since his time of a poetic genius so dedicated to God, it is that of Gerard Hopkins. We are certainly justified in presuming that no other subject-matter than that to which he confined himself could have elicited great poetry from George Herbert. Whether we regard this as a limitation, or as the sign of solitary greatness, of a unique contribution to English poetry, will depend upon our sensibility to the themes of which he writes.

It would, however, be a gross error to assume that Herbert's poems are of value only for Christians—or, still more narrowly, only for members of his own church. For the practising Christian, it is true, they may be aids to devotion. When I claim a place for Herbert among those poets whose work every lover of English poetry should read and every student of English poetry should study, irrespective of religious belief or unbelief, I am not thinking primarily of the exquisite craftmanship, the extraordinary metrical virtuosity, or the verbal felicities, but of the *content* of the poems which make up *The Temple*. These poems form a record of spiritual struggle which should touch the feeling, and enlarge the understanding of those readers also who hold no religious belief and find themselves unmoved by religious emotion. Professor L. C. Knights, in an essay on George Herbert in his *Explorations*, both expresses this doubt on the part of the non-Christian and dispels it:

> Even Dr. Hutchinson, whose superbly edited and annotated edition of the Complete Works is not likely to be superseded . . . remarks that 'if to-day there is a less general sympathy with Herbert's religion, the beauty and sincerity of its expression are appreciated by those who do not share it'. True, but there is much more than the 'expression' that we appreciate, as I shall try to show. Herbert's poetry is an integral part of the great English tradition.

Whether the religious poems of Donne show greater profundity of thought, and greater intensity of passion, is a question which every reader will answer according to his own feelings. My point here is that *The Temple* is not to be regarded simply as a collection of poems, but (as I have said,) as a record of the spiritual struggles of a man of intellectual power and emotional intensity who gave much toil to perfecting his verses. As such, it should be a document of interest to all those who are curious to understand their fellow men; and as such, I regard it as a more important document than all of Donne's *religious* poems taken together.

On the other hand, I find Herbert to be closer in spirit to Donne than is any other of 'the school of Donne'. As the personal bond, through Lady Herbert, was much closer, this seems only natural. Other powerful literary influences formed the manner of Crashaw, the Roman Catholic convert: the Italian poet Marino and the Spanish poet Gongora, and, we are told,[1] the Jesuit poets who wrote in Latin. Vaughan and Traherne were poets of mystical experience: each appears to have experienced early in life some mystical illumination which inspires his poetry. And the other important poet of the 'metaphysical' school, Andrew Marvell, is a master of secular and religious poetry equally. In my attempt to indicate the affinity of Herbert to Donne, and also the difference between them, I have spoken earlier of a 'balance' between the intellect and the sensibility. But equally well (for one has recourse to diverse and even mutually contradictory metaphors and images to express the inexpressible) we can speak of a 'fusion' of intellect and sensibility in different proportions. In the work of a later generation of 'metaphysicals'—notably Cleveland, Benlowes and Cowley—we encounter a kind of emotional drought, and a verbal ingenuity which, having no great depth of feeling to work upon, tends towards corruption of language,

---

[1] By Mario Praz, whose *Seicentismo e marinismo in Inghilterra* is essential for the study of Crashaw in particular.

and merits the censure which Samuel Johnson applies indiscriminately to all the 'school of Donne'.

To return to the import of *The Temple* for all perceptive readers whether they share Herbert's faith or no. Professor Knights quotes with approval Dr. Hutchinson's description of the poems as

> colloquies of the soul with God or self-communings which seek to bring order into that complex personality of his which he analyses so unsparingly,

but goes on to make a qualification which seems to me very important. Dr. Hutchinson believes that Herbert's principal temptation was *ambition*. We need not deny that Herbert had been, like many other men, ambitious; we know that he had a hot temper; we know that he liked fine clothes and fine company, and would have been pleased by preferment at Court. But beside the struggle to abandon thought of the attractions offered to worldly ambition, Professor Knights finds 'a dejection of spirit that tended to make him regard his own life, the life he was actually leading, as worthless and unprofitable'. Mr. Knights attributes the cause partly to ill-health, but still more to a *more ingrained distrust*. It was perhaps distrust of himself, or fear of testing his powers among more confident men, that drove him to the shelter of an obscure parsonage. He had, Mr. Knights suggests, to rid himself of the torturing sense of frustration and impotence and accept the validity of his own experience. If this is so, Herbert's weakness became the source of his greatest power, for the result was *The Temple*.

I have called upon Mr. Knights's testimony in evidence that Herbert is not a poet whose work is significant only for Christian readers; that *The Temple* is not to be taken as simply a devotional handbook of meditation for the faithful, but as the personal record of a man very conscious of weakness and failure, a man of intellect and sensibility who hungered and thirsted after righteousness. And that by its *content*, as well as because of its technical accomplishment, it is a work of importance for every lover of poetry. This is not, however, to suggest that it is unprofitable for us to study the text for closer understanding, to acquaint ourselves with the liturgy of the Church, with the traditional imagery of the Church, and identify the Biblical allusions. One long poem which has been subjected to close examination is 'The Sacrifice'. There are sixty-three stanzas of three lines each, sixty-one of which have the refrain 'Was ever grief like Mine?' I mention this poem, which is a very fine one, and not so familiar as are some of the shorter and more lyrical pieces, because it has been carefully studied by Professor William Empson in his *Seven Types of Ambiguity*, and by Miss Rosamund Tuve in her *A Reading of George Herbert*. The lines are to be taken as spoken by Christ upon the Cross. We need, of course, enough acquaintance with the New Testament to recognise references to the Passion. But we are also better prepared if we recognise the Lamentations of Jeremiah, and the Reproaches in the Mass of the Presanctified which is celebrated on Good Friday.

> *Celebrant:* I led thee forth out of Egypt, drowning Pharaoh in the Red Sea: and thou hast delivered me up unto the chief priests.
> *Deacon & Subdeacon:* O my people, what have I done unto thee, or wherein have I wearied thee? Testify against me.

It is interesting to note that Mr. Empson and Miss Tuve differ in their interpretation of the following stanza:

> O all ye who passe by, behold and see;
> Man stole the fruit, but I must climbe the tree;
> The tree of life to all, but onely me:
>
> > Was ever grief like mine?

Mr. Empson comments: 'He climbs the tree to repay what was stolen, as if he were putting the apple back'; and develops this explanation at some length. Upon this interpretation Miss Tuve observes rather tartly: 'All (Mr. Empson's) rabbits roll out of one small hat—the fact that

Herbert uses the time-honoured 'climb' for the ascent of the Cross, and uses the word 'must', to indicate a far deeper necessity than that which faces a small boy under a big tree.' Certainly, the image of *replacing* the apple which has been plucked is too ludicrous to be entertained for a moment. It is obvious that Christ 'climbs' or is 'lifted' up on the Cross in atonement for the sin of Adam and Eve; the verb 'climb' being used traditionally to indicate the *voluntary* nature of the sacrifice for the sins of the world. Herbert was, assuredly, familiar with the imagery used by the pre-Reformation Church. It is likely also that Donne, learned in the works of the scholastics, and also in the writings of such Roman theologians contemporary with himself as Cardinal Bellarmine, set a standard of scholarship which Herbert followed.

To cite such an instance as this, however, is not to suggest that the lover of poetry needs to prepare himself with theological and liturgical knowledge *before* approaching Herbert's poetry. That would be to put the cart before the horse. With the appreciation of Herbert's poems, as with all poetry, enjoyment is the beginning as well as the end. We must enjoy the poetry before we attempt to penetrate the poet's mind; we must enjoy it before we understand it, if the attempt to understand it is to be worth the trouble. We begin by enjoying poems, and lines in poems, which make an immediate impression; only gradually, as we familiarise ourselves with the whole work, do we appreciate *The Temple* as a coherent sequence of poems setting down the fluctuations of emotion between despair and bliss, between agitation and serenity, and the discipline of suffering which leads to peace of spirit.

The relation of enjoyment to belief—the question whether a poem has more to give us if we share the beliefs of its author, is one which has never been answered satisfactorily: the present writer has made some attempt to contribute to the solution of the problem, and remains dissatisfied with his attempts. But one thing is certain: that even if the reader enjoys a poem more fully when he shares the beliefs of the

author, he will miss a great deal of possible enjoyment
and of valuable experience if he does not seek the fullest
understanding possible of poetry in reading which he must
'suspend his disbelief'. (The present writer is very thankful
for having had the opportunity to study the *Bhagavad Gītā*
and the religious and philosophical beliefs, so different
from his own, with which the *Bhagavad Gītā* is informed.)

Some of the poems in *The Temple* express moods of
anguish and sense of defeat or failure:

> At first thou gav'st me milk and sweetnesses;
>> I had my wish and way:
> My dayes were straw'd with flow'rs and happinesse;
>> There was no moneth but May.
> But with my yeares sorrow did twist and grow,
> And made a partie unawares for wo. . . .
>
> Yet, though thou troublest me, I must be meek;
>> In weaknesse must be stout.
> Well, I will change the service, and go seek
>> Some other master out.
> Ah my deare God! though I am clean forgot,
> Let me not love thee, if I love thee not.

The foregoing lines are from the first of five poems all of
which bear the title 'Affliction'. In the first of two poems
both of which are entitled 'The Temper', he speaks of his
fluctuations of faith and feeling:

> How should I praise thee, Lord! how should my rymes
>> Gladly engrave thy love in steel,
> If what my soul doth feel sometimes,
>> My soul might ever feel!

The great danger, for the poet who would write religious
verse, is that of setting down what he would like to feel
rather than be faithful to the expression of what he really
feels. Of such pious insincerity Herbert is never guilty. We

need not look too narrowly for a steady progress in Herbert's religious life, in an attempt to discover a chronological order. He falls, and rises again. Also, he was accustomed to working over his poems; they may have circulated in manuscript among his intimates during his lifetime. What we can confidently believe is that every poem in the book is true to the poet's experience. In some poems there is a more joyous note, as in 'Whitsunday':

> Listen sweet Dove unto my song,
> And spread thy golden wings in me;
> Hatching my tender heart so long,
> Till it get wing, and flie away with thee. . . .
>
> Lord, though we change, thou art the same;
> The same sweet God of love and light:
> Restore this day, for thy great name,
> Unto his ancient and miraculous right.

In 'The Flower' we hear the note of serenity, almost of beatitude, and of thankfulness for God's blessings:

> How fresh, O Lord, how sweet and clean
> Are thy returns! ev'n as the flowers in spring;
> To which, besides their own demean,
> The late-past frosts tributes of pleasure bring.
> Grief melts away
> Like snow in May,
> As if there were no such cold thing.
>
> . . . . . .
>
> And now in age I bud again,
> After so many deaths I live and write;
> I once more smell the dew and rain,
> And relish versing: O my onely light,
> It cannot be
> That I am he
> On whom thy tempests fell all night.[1]

[1] A. Alvarez in *The School of Donne* says justly of this stanza: 'This is, I suppose, the most perfect and most vivid stanza in the whole of Herbert's work. But it is, in every sense, so natural that its originality is easily missed.' (See also Coleridge on this poem: footnote to p.10.)

I cannot resist the thought that in this last stanza—itself a miracle of phrasing—the imagery, so apposite to express the achievement of faith which it records, is taken from the experience of the man of delicate physical health who had known much illness. It is on this note of joy in convalescence of the spirit in surrender to God, that the life of discipline of this haughty and irascible Herbert finds conclusion: *In His will is our peace.*

III

Of all the 'school of Donne' Herbert is the closest to the old Master. Two other fine poets of the group might just as well be said to belong to the 'school of Herbert'. The debt of Vaughan to Herbert can be shown by quotation; Herbert's most recent and authoritative editor, Dr. F. E. Hutchinson, says: 'there is no example in English literature of one poet adopting another poet's work so extensively.' As for Crashaw, he undoubtedly admired Herbert. Nevertheless, in spite of a continuity of influence and inspiration, we must remember that these four poets, who form a constellation of religious genius unparalleled in English poetry, are all highly individual, and very different from each other.

The resemblances and differences between Donne and Herbert are peculiarly fascinating. I have suggested earlier that the difference between the poetry of Donne and Herbert shows some parallel to the difference between their careers in the Church. Donne the Dean of St. Paul's, whose sermons drew crowds in the City of London; Herbert the shepherd of a little flock of rustics, to whom he laboured to explain the meaning of the rites of the Church, the significance of Holy Days, in language that they could understand. There are, however, lines which might have come from either, where we seem to hear the same voice— Herbert echoing the idiom or reflecting the imagery of Donne. There is at least one poem of Herbert's in which he plays with extended metaphor in the manner of Donne.

It is 'Obedience' where he uses legal terms almost through-
out:

> My God, if writings may
> Convey a Lordship any way
> Whither the buyer and the seller please;
> Let it not thee displease,
> If this poore paper do as much as they.

. . . . .

> He that will passe his land,
> As I have mine, may set his hand
> And heart unto this Deed, when he hath read;
> And make the purchase spread
> To both our goods, if he to it will stand.

Such elaboration is not typical of Herbert. But there is *wit*
like that of Donne in 'The Quip'. One feels obliged to quote
the whole poem:

> The merrie world did on a day
> With his train-bands and mates agree
> To meet together, where I lay,
> And all in sport to geere at me.

> First, Beautie crept into a rose,
> Which when I pluckt not, Sir, said she,
> Tell me, I pray, Whose hands are those?
> *But thou shalt answer, Lord, for me.*

> Then Money came, and chinking still,
> What tune is this, poore man? said he:
> I heard in Musick you had skill.
> *But thou shalt answer, Lord, for me.*

> Then came brave Glorie puffing by
> In silks that whistled, who but he?
> He scarce allow'd me half an eie.
> *But thou shalt answer, Lord, for me.*

> Then came quick Wit and Conversation,
> And he would needs a comfort be,
> And, to be short, make an Oration.
> *But thou shalt answer, Lord, for me.*

Yet when the houre of thy designe
To answer these fine things shall come;
Speak not at large; say, I am thine:
And then they have their answer home.

Professor Knights observes very shrewdly: 'the personifi-
cations here have nothing in common with Spenser's
allegorical figures or with the capitalised abstractions of the
eighteenth century: "brave Glorie puffing by in silks that
whistled" might have come straight from *The Pilgrim's
Progress*.' How audible are these silks 'that whistled'!
'Puffing' is equally apt: the same participle is used, to
produce another but equally striking effect, elsewhere:

Sometimes Death, puffing at the doore,
Blows all the dust about the floore.

(*The Church Floore*)

Herbert is a master of the simple everyday word in the
right place, and charges it with concentrated meaning, as
in 'Redemption', one of the poems known to all readers
of anthologies:

Having been tenant long to a rich Lord,
    Not thriving, I resolved to be bold,
    And make a suit unto him, to afford
A new small-rented lease, and cancell th'old.
In heaven at his manour I him sought:
    They told me there, that he was lately gone
    About some land, which he had dearly bought
Long since on earth, to take possession.
I straight return'd, and knowing his great birth,
    Sought him accordingly in great resorts;
    In cities, theatres, gardens, parks, and courts:
At length I heard a ragged noise and mirth
    Of theeves and murderers: there I him espied,
    Who straight, *Your suit is granted*, said, & died.

The phrase 'ragged noise and mirth' gives us, in four words,
the picture of the scene to which Herbert wishes to intro-
duce us.

There are many lines which remind us of Donne:

> What though my bodie runne to dust?
> Faith cleaves unto it, counting evr'y grain
> With an exact and most particular trust,
>   Reserving all for flesh again.
>   (*Faith*)

> My God, what is a heart?
>   Silver, or gold, or precious stone,
>   Or starre, or rainbow, or a part
> Of all these things, or all of them in one?
>   (*Mattens*)

>   . . . learn here thy stemme
> And true descent; that when thou shalt grow fat,

> And wanton in thy cravings, thou mayst know,
> That flesh is but the glasse, which holds the dust
> That measures all our time; which also shall
> Be crumbled into dust. . . .
>   (*Church-monuments*)

> Lord, how can man preach thy eternall word ?
>   He is a brittle crazie glasse: . . .
>   (*The Windows*)

> My bent thoughts, like a brittle bow,
>   Did flie asunder: . . .
>   (*Deniall*)

Herbert must have learned from Donne the cunning use of both the learned and the common word, to give the sudden shock of surprise and delight.

> But man is close, reserv'd, and dark to thee:
>   When thou demandest but a heart,
>   He cavils instantly.
>   In his poore cabinet of bone
>   Sinnes have their box apart,
> Defrauding thee, who gavest two for one.
>   (*Ungratefulnesse*)

> The fleet Astronomer can bore,
> And thred the spheres with his quick-piercing minde:
> He views their stations, walks from doore to doore,
> Surveys, as if he had design'd
> To make a purchase there: he sees their dances,
> And knoweth long before
> Both their full-ey'd aspects, and secret glances.
> (*Vanitie*)

> My thoughts are all a case of knives, . . .
> (*Affliction IV.*)

The following lines are very reminiscent of Donne:

> How soon doth man decay!
> When clothes are taken from a chest of sweets
> To swaddle infants, whose young breath
> Scarce knows the way;
> Those clouts are little winding sheets,
> Which do consigne and send them unto death.
> (*Mortification*)

Here and there one can believe that Herbert has uncon-
sciously used a word, or a rhythm of Donne, in a very
different context from that of the original, as perhaps in the
first line of 'The Discharge':

> Busie enquiring heart, what wouldst thou know?

Donne begins 'The Sunne Rising' with the line

> Busie old foole, unruly Sunne. . .

If Herbert's line be an echo and not a mere coincidence—
the reader must form his own opinion—it is all the more
interesting because of the difference in subject matter between
the two poems. If Herbert, in writing a poem of religious
mortification, could echo a poem of Donne which is an
aubade of the lover's complaint that day should come so

soon, it suggests that the literary influence of the elder man
upon the younger was profound indeed.

Herbert's metrical forms, however, are both original and
varied. To have invented and perfected so many variations
in the form of lyrical verse is evidence of native genius,
hard work and a passion for perfection. Two of his poems
are such as would be considered, if written by a poet to-day,
merely elegant trifles: 'The Altar' and 'Easter Wings'. In
each, there is a disposition of longer and shorter lines so
printed that the poem has the shape, the one of an altar and
the other of a pair of wings. Such a diversion, if employed
frequently, would be tedious, distracting and trying to the
eyesight and we must be glad that Herbert did not make
further use of these devices: yet it is evidence of Herbert's
care for workmanship, his restless exploration of variety,
and of a kind of gaiety of spirit, a joy in composition which
engages our delighted sympathy. The exquisite variations of
form in the other poems of *The Temple* show a resourceful-
ness of invention which seems inexhaustible, and for which
I know no parallel in English poetry. Here, we can only
quote a stanza from each of a brief selection to suggest the
astonishing variety:

> O my chief good,
> How shall I measure out thy bloud?
> How shall I count what thee befell,
> And each grief tell?
>> (*Good Friday*)

> O blessed bodie! Whither are thou thrown?
> No lodging for thee, but a cold hard stone?
> So many hearts on earth, and yet not one
>> Receive thee?
>> (*Sepulchre*)

Poems in such measures as these, and more obviously 'The
Sacrifice', which we have quoted earlier, seem to indicate
an ear trained by the music of liturgy.

Rise heart; thy Lord is risen. Sing his praise
Without delayes,
Who takes thee by the hand, that thou likewise
With him mayst rise:
That, as his death calcined thee to dust,
His life may make thee gold, and much more, just.
(*Easter*)

The slow movement of the last line quoted above has something of the movement of the exquisite line which ends Donne's 'Nocturnall upon S. Lucies Day':

Both the yeares, and the dayes deep midnight is.

Somewhat similar to the movement of 'Good Friday' (quoted above) is:

Since, Lord, to thee
A narrow way and little gate
Is all the passage, on my infancie
Thou didst lay hold, and antedate
My faith in me.
(*Holy Baptisme I*)

Close enough to the form of 'Holy Baptisme' for its difference to be all the more striking is:

Lord, I confesse my sinne is great;
Great is my sinne. Oh! gently treat
With thy quick flow'r, thy momentarie bloom;
Whose life still pressing
Is one undressing,
A steadie aiming at a tombe.
(*Repentance*)

The next quotation has a solemn liturgical movement suited to the subject-matter and the title:

O Do not use me
After my sinnes! look not on my desert,
But on thy glorie! then thou wilt reform
And not refuse me: for thou onely art
The mightie God, but I a sillie worm;
O do not bruise me!
(*Sighs and Grones*)

Herbert knows the effect of denying a rhyme where it is expected:

When my devotions could not pierce
Thy silent eares;
Then was my heart broken, as was my verse:
My breast was full of fears
And disorder:
(*Deniall*)

The roughness of metre of the line

Then was my heart broken, as was my verse

is exactly what is wanted to convey the meaning of the words. The following stanza has an apparent artlessness and conversational informality which only a great artist could achieve:

Lord, let the Angels praise thy name.
Man is a foolish thing, a foolish thing,
Folly and Sinne play all his game.
His house still burns, and yet he still doth sing,
Man is but grasse,
He knows it, fill the glasse.
(*Miserie*)

The next poem to be quoted is one of several poems of Herbert which, while being, like all the rest of his work, personal, have been set to music and sung as hymns:

King of Glorie, King of Peace,
I will love thee:
And that love may never cease,
I will move thee.
(*Praise II*)

The same masterly simplicity is visible in:

> Throw away thy rod,
> Throw away thy wrath:
>   O my God,
> Take the gentle path.
>
> (*Discipline*)

I wish to end by giving in full the poem which, significantly, I think, ends *The Temple*. It is named 'Love III', and indicates the serenity finally attained by this proud and humble man:

> Love bade me welcome: yet my soul drew back,
>   Guiltie of dust and sinne.
> But quick-ey'd Love, observing me grow slack
>   From my first entrance in,
> Drew nearer to me, sweetly questioning,
>   If I lack'd any thing.
>
> A guest, I answer'd, worthy to be here:
>   Love said, You shall be he.
> I the unkinde, ungratefull? Ah my deare,
>   I cannot look on thee.
> Love took my hand, and smiling did reply,
>   Who made the eyes but I?
>
> Truth Lord, but I have marr'd them: let my shame
>   Go where it doth deserve.
> And know you not, sayes Love, who bore the blame?
>   My deare, then I will serve.
> You must sit down, sayes Love, and taste my meat:
>   So I did sit and eat.

GEORGE HERBERT

A Select Bibliography

(Place of publication London, unless stated otherwise)

Bibliography:

A HERBERT BIBLIOGRAPHY, by G. H. Palmer. Cambridge, Mass. (1911)
—a privately printed catalogue of the compiler's collection of books by and about Herbert. Useful but incomplete.

Collected Editions:

THE WORKS, with a Preface by W. Pickering and Notes by S. T. Coleridge. 2 vols. (1835-6).

THE COMPLETE WORKS, edited by A. B. Grosart. 3 vols. (1874)
—textually most unreliable, but the first edition to make use of the Williams MS.

THE ENGLISH WORKS NEWLY ARRANGED, edited by G. H. Palmer. 3 vols. (1905-1907)
—an important edition, notwithstanding some editorial liberties and speculations.

WORKS, edited by F. E. Hutchinson. Oxford (1941)
—the definitive edition in the Oxford English Texts Series. The World's Classics reprint, 1961, has a valuable introduction by H. Gardner.

Separate Works:

THE TEMPLE, SACRED POEMS AND PRIVATE EJACULATIONS, Cambridge (1633)
—13 editions were published before 1709 but none thereafter until 1799. The Nonesuch Press edition (1927) edited by F. Meynell (with a bibliographical note by G. Keynes) is based on the Bodleian MS (Tanner 307) which was the copy licensed in 1633 for the printer by the Cambridge Vice-Chancellor and his assessors.

WITTS RECREATIONS. WITH A THOUSAND OUTLANDISH PROVERBS SELECTED BY MR. G. H. (1640)
—the proverbs attributed to Herbert were published separately in 1651 as *Jacula Prudentum*.

HERBERT'S REMAINS (1652)
—contains most of *A Priest to the Temple* and *Jacula Prudentum*.

A PRIEST TO THE TEMPLE, OR, THE COUNTREY PARSON HIS CHARACTER, AND RULE OF HOLY LIFE (1671)
—a selection, edited by G. M. Forbes, was published in 1949.

Herbert contributed Latin and Greek poems to the following memorial collections: *Epicedium Cantabrigiense, in Obitum Henrici Principis Walliae*. Cambridge, 1612 (2 Latin poems); *Lacrymae Cantabrigienses, in Obitum Reginae Annae*. Cambridge, 1619 (1 Latin poem); *True Copies of all the Latine Orations, made at Cambridge on the 25 and 27 of Februarie last past*, 1623 (1 Latin oration with English translation); *Oratio qua Principis Caroli Reditum ex Hispaniis Celebravit Georgius Herbert*. Cambridge, 1623 (1 Latin oration); *Memoriae Francisci, Baronis de Verulamio, Sacrum*, 1626 (1 Latin poem); *A Sermon of Commemoration of the Lady Danvers by John Donne. Together with other Commemorations of her, called Parentalia by her Sonne, G. Herbert*, 1627 (19 Latin and Greek poems).

Some Critical and Biographical Studies:

THE LIFE OF LORD HERBERT OF CHERBURY (1764)
—see also Lord Herbert's *Poems*, edited Moore Smith, Oxford, 1923.
THE LIFE OF MR. GEORGE HERBERT, by I. Walton (1670)
—reprinted in Walton's *Lives*, 1670 (World's Classics edition, 1923).
BIOGRAPHIA LITERARIA, by S. T. Coleridge (1817)
—chapters XIX and XX.
METAPHYSICAL POEMS AND LYRICS OF THE SEVENTEENTH CENTURY, edited with an introduction by H. Grierson. Oxford (1921).
SEICENTISMO E MARINISMO IN INGHILTERRA, di M. Praz. Florence (1925).
A CONCORDANCE TO THE ENGLISH POEMS, by C. Mann. Boston, Mass. (1927).
SEVEN TYPES OF AMBIGUITY, by W. Empson (1930).
THE DONNE TRADITION, by G. Williamson. Cambridge, Mass. (1930).
FOUR METAPHYSICAL POETS, by J. Bennett. Cambridge (1934; revised edition, 1953).
THE METAPHYSICAL POETS, by J. B. Leishman. Oxford (1934).
EXPLORATION: ESSAYS IN LITERARY CRITICISM, by L. C. Knights (1946)
—contains his essay on Herbert first printed in *Scrutiny*, 1933.
A READING OF GEORGE HERBERT, by R. Tuve. Chicago (1952).
GEORGE HERBERT, by M. Bottrall (1954).
GEORGE HERBERT, by J. H. Summers. Cambridge, Mass. (1954).
TWO GENTLE MEN, by M. Chute. New York (1959)
—biographies of Herbert and Herrick. English edition, 1960.
THE SCHOOL OF DONNE, by A. Alvarez (1961).